FRIENDSHIP AND FREEDOM:
The Story of the Statue of Liberty

American Icons Series Book One

FRIENDSHIP AND FREEDOM:
The Story of the Statue of Liberty

JANICE WILHELM

Wildrose Media

Friendship and Freedom: The Story of the Statue of Liberty

No part of this publication may be reproduced, stored, or transmitted in any form or by any means, electronic, mechanical, photocopying, recording, scanning, or otherwise without written permission from the publisher. It is illegal to copy this book, post it to a website, or distribute it by any other means without permission.

Janice Wilhelm has no responsibility for the persistence of URLs for external or third-party Internet Websites referred to in this publication and does not guarantee that any content on such Websites is, or will remain, accurate or appropriate.

Text Copyright ©2020 Wildrose Media. All rights reserved.

Published in the United States of America by Wildrose Media.

www.wildrose-media.com

Cataloging-in-Publication Data filed with the Library of Congress.

Paperback ISBN: 978-1-7327803-9-2

ePUB ISBN: 978-1-7327803-8-5

First Edition

Friendship and Freedom:
The Story of the Statue of Liberty

INTRODUCTION	9
IMMIGRATION; HOPE FOR A NEW LIFE	11
ACROSS THE OCEAN	15
INSPIRATION	17
AN IDEA TAKES SHAPE; THE STATUE'S DESIGN	19
The Colossus Of Rhodes	21
A VISIT TO AMERICA	23
Bedloe's Island	24
RETURN TO FRANCE	27
CONSTRUCTION BEGINS	29
A PRETTY, YET PRACTICAL EXTERIOR	33
Copper	35
THE STATUE'S INTERIOR	37
Eiffel Tower	39
SHARING THE COST; THE FUNDRAISING BEGINS	41
LIBERTY ON DISPLAY IN AMERICA	43
1876 Centennial Exposition In Philadelphia	46
PERMISSION GRANTED	49
FUNDRAISING IN AMERICA	51
THE PEDESTAL	55
PULITZER'S CROWDFUNDING CAMPAIGN	59
A Gift For Frederic Bartholdi	60
ASSEMBLY IN FRANCE	61
THE PEDESTAL IS COMPLETE	63
A NEW HOME	65
The Isere	68
LIBERTY ENLIGHTENING THE WORLD	69
Ticker Tape Parades	71

LIGHTING THE TORCH	73
CONTROVERSY	75
SYMBOLISM	77
THE POEM	79
MAINTENANCE AND RESTORATION	81
1916	81
The 1930s	82
The 1980s	82
Liberty Weekend July 1986	85
The 2000s	86
CONCLUSION	88
STATUE OF LIBERTY FACTS	89
THE PEOPLE BEHIND THE STATUE	91
Frédéric Auguste Bartholdi	91
Alexandre-Gustave Eiffel	92
Albert Fernique	93
Richard Morris Hunt	94
Édouard René Lefebvre de Laboulaye	95
Emma Lazarus	96
Joseph Pulitzer	97
TIMELINE	99
THE NEW COLOSSUS	105
DID YOU KNOW…?	107
GLOSSARY OF TERMS	111
QUESTIONS FROM THE BOOK	113
BIBLIOGRAPHY	115
NOTES	121
ALSO BY JANICE WILHELM	123

Dedicated with love to my grandparents, Lambertus & Johanna Roscher and Frederick & Albertje Talen, who bravely sought a better life for their families in a foreign land.

INTRODUCTION

Known as the city that never sleeps, New York is an energetic blend of food, fashion, and cultural diversity. A popular travel destination, each year millions of visitors come to experience all that the city has to offer. Popular tourist attractions include Times Square, Central Park, Broadway, and the Empire State Building. Those who dare, enjoy a ride in one of New York's legendary yellow cabs.

Right outside the hustle and bustle of the city, on a small island off the tip of Manhattan, stands the statue of a woman. Clothed in a robe and wearing a crown, she proudly holds her torch high, welcoming citizens and visitors alike. Each year, over four million people from across the globe board ferries to visit this iconic symbol of America and her sister island, Ellis. Unique among American monuments, Lady Liberty, as she is affectionately known, does not commemorate a person, but an ideal.

This is her story.

Image source: Max Pexels, CC0 license.

IMMIGRATION; HOPE FOR A NEW LIFE

★ ★ ★

Many years ago, before the convenience of commercial airplanes, people crossed the ocean by boat. In the mid to late 1800s thousands of people left their homes in Europe or Asia to begin a new life in America. For these immigrants, the United States was a land full of promise and opportunity. These people left their homes to escape terrible living conditions, including poverty, war, or famine. Some sought safety from corrupt governments or religious persecution.

Amidst tearful goodbyes, these brave men, women, and children boarded ships destined for North America. The journey across the Atlantic Ocean was long and often difficult as the passengers endured heartache, storms, even illness. To those willing to risk it all, America offered renewed hope and the promise of a better tomorrow.

Immigrants on deck of the steamship Germanic, 1886.
Image: Wikimedia commons, public domain.

Once the ship had docked, her passengers disembarked and were directed to an immigration center—the place where their future in America was determined. Not all who arrived would be permitted to stay.

New arrivals stood in line for many hours, awaiting inspection. First their names were checked, and documents were verified. Most immigrants did not understand, speak, or read English, which made communication difficult. Occasionally families were separated, causing additional anxiety and stress.

Next, they were examined for illness and disease. Those deemed unfit or incurable were returned to the ship and forced to endure the long journey home. Those deemed curable were housed in medical facilities, isolated from their loved ones. The people who arrived healthy and strong were transported to the mainland to begin their new life—often with nothing but the clothes on their backs and a determination to succeed. The immigrants faced an uncertain future in an unfamiliar land.

Beginning in 1892, Ellis Island held the main processing center for European immigrants entering the United States. Ellis Island sits in the New York Bay, near Bedloe's Island and Governor's Island. As the immigrant ships steamed into the Bay, the people onboard caught their first glimpse of America. On Bedloe's Island an enormous figure held her torch high, greeting the new arrivals. At her feet lay a broken chain, indicating to all who passed freedom from the bondage of their prior lives. The Statue of Liberty signaled renewed hope and a fresh beginning.

Though immigrants now enter the United States through various locations, millions of people visit New York each year. As a favorite tourist destination, Lady Liberty is well-loved and admired worldwide. However, this universal appeal was not always the case.

The Statue of Liberty was not immediately embraced by the American people. Initially, she faced disinterest from a nation attempting to recover from its bloodiest war. As time progressed, the attitude toward her changed. Gradually adopted into the hearts of the American people, she now stands proudly—a symbol of American values and freedoms. She has been pictured on advertising, postage stamps, military recruitment posters, and even currency.

Stamp, 1922. Public domain.

The Statue of Liberty possesses a remarkable history. Over the years she has weathered protests, storms, wars, renovations, and repairs. Her tenacity and strength during adversity demonstrate to the world what it means to be American.

As one of America's most well-known symbols, many are surprised to discover that this familiar icon was once an immigrant herself! She was a gift from France to commemorate the 100th anniversary of the signing of the Declaration of Independence.

ACROSS THE OCEAN
★ ★ ★

France, a country in Europe, is located directly across the English Channel from Great Britain, immediately north of Spain. Though at peace now, many years ago, France and Great Britain were enemies. The two countries fought over territory in Europe and abroad.

During the American Revolution, France became America's first ally. The thirteen colonies in America fought this war to gain independence from Great Britain. The American colonists were tired of paying taxes to British legislators who did not have America's best interests at heart. The colonists decided to fight for the right to govern themselves. This Revolutionary War was fought from 1775-1783.

Happy to fight against the British, France provided the beleaguered colonists with soldiers, ships, and supplies. France's support was instrumental in the successful outcome of the war. The colonists' victory over Great Britain led to the birth of this nation now known as the United States. The colonists, now called Americans, were extremely grateful to France for its help, and a strong friendship developed between the two nations.

The Battle of the Chesapeake, 1781. France defeated Britain.
Image - public domain.

France itself had experienced an unsettled government. Originally voted into power in 1848, Napoleon III governed as President of France. Discovering he was ineligible for a second term; Napoleon III changed the laws to declare himself emperor. He was an authoritarian ruler.

During the Franco-Prussian War of 1870-71, Napoleon III was captured. France was briefly governed by a radical socialist group, which the French military defeated.

In 1870 the people of France were divided over whether to establish a republic or a monarchist-style government. As a result of the controversy, France adopted a provisional government—a series of temporary leaders.

Eventually a compromise was reached. The Comte de Chambord, a descendant of King Charles X, was crowned as France's King Henry V. Despite the installment of the new king, the political turmoil continued—especially over the French flag. King Henry V and his supporters wished to change it; others disagreed. A temporary republic government was established, which allowed the king to keep his position. Though plans were made to appoint a more liberal king after Henry V died, this did not happen. By the time of Henry V's death in 1883, the French people had tired of the monarchy, choosing to remain a democracy instead. This political unrest prompted influential French citizens to seriously consider adopting the American style of government.

France eventually established a Republican Parliamentary Democracy, with a constitution like that of the United States.

INSPIRATION
★ ★ ★

The idea of presenting a gift to the United States came from a citizen of France, Mr. Édouard René Lefebvre de Laboulaye. A French politician and author, Mr. Laboulaye loved American ideals. He had studied America's history and was a dedicated supporter of democracy. As an anti-slavery activist, he applauded President Lincoln's Emancipation Proclamation and was impressed by Lincoln's ability to reunite the Northern and Southern states following America's bitter Civil War.

On April 21, 1865, a group of pro-American men gathered at Mr. Laboulaye's home near Versailles, France. These wealthy and educated men met to celebrate the end of the U.S. Civil War and the abolition of slavery in America. The meeting had a somber atmosphere, for they mourned America's President, Abraham Lincoln. President Lincoln had died from an assassin's bullet only six days earlier.

President Abraham Lincoln. Photo by Alexander Gardner, 1863. Public domain.

Funeral of President Lincoln. Harper's Bazaar May 6, 1865. Public domain.

As president of the gathered French Emancipation Committee, Mr. Laboulaye delivered an emotional speech. In this speech he presented the idea of giving a special gift to the United States. This gift would both commemorate the end of slavery in America and celebrate the enduring friendship between the two nations.

In secret, these men understood that this gift was also a silent protest of France's current ruler, Napoleon III, and his authoritarian rule. Édouard Laboulaye and his group hoped to inspire their fellow French citizens to demand a democratic-style government. They believed a monument commemorating America's triumph over its hardships would inspire the French citizens.

AN IDEA TAKES SHAPE; THE STATUE'S DESIGN

★★★

One of the dinner guests was a young sculptor and friend of Édouard Laboulaye named Frédéric-Auguste Bartholdi. Mr. Bartholdi embraced the idea of presenting Americans with a present which commemorated the end of slavery. He had the perfect idea for the gift.

In the 1850s Mr. Bartholdi had visited Egypt and Yemen with several other artists. While there he fell in love with the giant statues outside the tombs at Abu Simbel. The sight of these immense monuments inspired Mr. Bartholdi to create large scale art himself. In fact, at the time of this dinner party, Mr. Bartholdi had already designed a huge lighthouse statue for Egypt.

Abu Simbel Temple
Photo credit: Pepaserbio, CC SA International 4.0 license.

A couple of years earlier, Egypt's leader, Khedive Ismail Pasha, had asked artists and engineers to submit their designs for a lighthouse to be placed at Port Said. The lighthouse would be located at the north end of the recently completed Suez Canal, a shipping channel connecting the Mediterranean Sea and the Red Sea, which enabled faster trade routes between Europe and Asia.

For Egypt's lighthouse, Frédéric Bartholdi had submitted a design proposal called *Egypt Carrying the Light to Asia*. Inspired by the ancient statue, *Colossus of Rhodes*, the design depicted an Arabian peasant woman wearing a veil and dressed in a robe. In her hand was a lantern which would serve as the beacon for the lighthouse. The completed statue would stand 86 feet tall (26 m) and be placed on a pedestal 48 feet (14.6 m) high. Together, the monument would tower 134 feet (40.8 m) above the coast.

Bartholdi's early designs for the Port Said Lighthouse.
Photo credit: Tian's Notebook 07-2015

Unfortunately for Mr. Bartholdi, his statue proved to be too expensive for the Egyptians, and his design was rejected. The less elaborate proposal of François Coignet was selected instead. His Port Said lighthouse was completed in 1869.

Port Said lighthouse, 1882.
Image: Wikimedia commons.

Seeing an opportunity to use his Egyptian design, Frederic Bartholdi eagerly shared his plans for the massive lighthouse with his friend, Édouard Laboulaye. Mr. Laboulaye approved of the idea. Modifying his original design, Bartholdi began to create the statue he named *La Liberté Éclaire la Monde* (*Liberty Enlightening the World*). Today she is affectionately known by the nickname *Statue of Liberty*.

Using historical art, including Libertas, the Roman goddess of freedom, Columbia, and Helios, the Greek sun god, as his inspiration, Mr. Bartholdi made several changes to his original lighthouse sketches. These changes included removing the veil from the statue's face and placing a crown upon her head.

Early drawings show the statue holding broken chains in her hand to symbolize the end of slavery. The Committee rejected this idea as too controversial. Though the Emancipation Act had been signed in 1865, not all of America's citizens agreed with the new law. Realizing the statue had to appeal to as many donors as possible, she was redesigned. The broken chain now lay under her feet, partially hidden by her robe.

Since this statue would stand near the water, it seemed fitting for her to remain a lighthouse. This purpose would make her practical as well as symbolic. The lantern was replaced with a torch.

One aspect of the statue's design receives ongoing debate: who was the inspiration behind her face? Many people believe the statue was modeled after Bartholdi's mother, while others claim it was a young girl he had seen during the Franco-Prussian War. Frédéric Bartholdi did not reveal the answer himself, so to this day the truth remains a mystery.

★★★

The Colossus Of Rhodes

The Colossus, one of the seven wonders of the ancient world, was a statue of the Greek sun god, Helios. Called the Colossus of Rhodes, it was built in 280 B.C. but destroyed by an earthquake a mere 56 years later. What is known about this statue is gleaned from historical accounts. According to these writings, the Colossus was constructed with an inner iron frame supporting a bronze outer layer, with two or three supporting inner columns made of stone. The statue, which stood nearly 110 feet (33.5 m) tall, guarded the harbor at Rhodes, an island near modern-day Turkey.

Artist's depiction of the Colossus of Rhodes.
Image – Wikimedia commons, public domain.

Often pictured standing with one leg on the island and the other on the mainland, this pose is unlikely for two reasons. First, the stance is not dignified enough for a god. Secondly, that position was impractical. To build such a large statue would require closing the harbor for years due to construction.

Following its destruction by an earthquake in 226 B.C., pieces of the Colossus lay in ruin for about 900 years. The statue's debris became an ancient tourist attraction. When Arabs conquered Rhodes in A.D. 654, the pieces of Colossus were cut apart and transported to Syria. There, the parts were melted down and re-purposed or sold.

A VISIT TO AMERICA
★ ★ ★

Work on the Statue of Liberty's design was placed on hold in 1870 when Frédéric Bartholdi was recruited to fight in the Franco-Prussian War. His hometown of Colmar was soon defeated. Sad and upset, Bartholdi retreated to the Bordeaux region of France.

Aware of his friend's unhappiness, Édouard Laboulaye encouraged Bartholdi to visit the United States. Bartholdi agreed, promising to scout a location for the statue to rest. He also made plans to solicit interest in the statue among the American people. Prior to leaving, Mr. Laboulaye gave Frédéric a list of influential men to contact during his stay.

Mr. Bartholdi arrived at New York Bay in June of 1871. As his ship sailed toward Manhattan, Bartholdi spotted the perfect location to house his Liberty statue—Bedloe's Island. This island was in the middle of New York Bay, between New Jersey and Brooklyn, about one mile off the southern tip of Manhattan. All ships destined for New York's ports traveled past this island as they sailed through the bay. Erected on this island, his statue would be prominently displayed. The location offered passengers on arriving ships their first glimpse of the United States. Bartholdi called this island "the gateway to America."

To be thorough in his search, Bartholdi examined other possible locations for the statue, including Central Park and Battery Park. Noting that the tall buildings would partially obscure the Statue, he concluded Bedloe's Island was indeed the best choice. From there his massive monument would be visible for miles in all directions.

Bedloe's Island

Bedloe's Island had undergone several owners and name changes by the time Frédéric Bartholdi noticed it. Originally owned by the Dutch, the island had been the property of the U.S. military for many years. During the War of 1812, Fort Wood had served as a key fortification used to protect New York from the British. The fort had been used during the Civil War as a hospital to care for Confederate prisoners of war. The fortifications were now unmanned and decaying.

Liberty Island (formerly Bedloe's Island) in New York Bay.
Image: Wikimedia commons, public domain.

Satisfied he had found the perfect location for the statue to rest, Bartholdi continued his travel within the United States. Touring by train from coast to coast, Mr. Bartholdi saw for himself the devastating damage caused by the Civil War. Roads, telegraph lines, and buildings were all in desperate need of repair. It appeared money was not available for art projects.

As promised, Bartholdi met with many influential, wealthy, and powerful people during his visit. These men included newspaper publishers, artists, writers, architects, senators. Along the way he met with Mormon leader

Brigham Young, poet Henry Wadsworth Longfellow, Charles Sumner, Frederick Olmstead, and even President Ulysses S. Grant.

Frédéric Bartholdi spoke with everyone he met about the statue but received a less-than-enthusiastic response. People seemed interested in the idea but were reluctant to commit money toward the project.

In Philadelphia, the statue's ideals had the support of the Union League Club. However, they failed to see the need for a physical structure to display them. America had been founded on freedom and self-government; these values were innate and a monument depicting them was not necessary. The Union League Club ultimately decided not to financially support Bartholdi's idea.

Disappointed but not discouraged, Frédéric Bartholdi traveled to Philadelphia. He stood in Independence Hall, where the Declaration of Independence had been signed. While there, he was informed that a huge celebration was planned for 1886, to mark the document's 100th anniversary. Bartholdi decided this event would be the perfect occasion to present France's special gift.

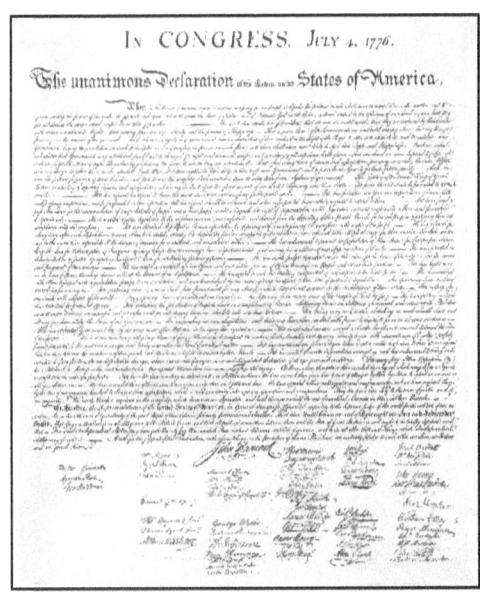

Declaration of Independence, 1823 William Stone facsimile. Image source: public domain.

RETURN TO FRANCE

★★★

Back home in France, Frédéric Bartholdi now focused on bringing his design to life. He had the full support of the Franco-American Union (Union Franco-Americaine), a group formed in 1875. Members included wealthy and important French citizens and Americans who chose to live in France. Dedicated to the ideals of liberty, independence, and democracy, this group's primary purpose was to see Bartholdi's statue completed.

The Franco-American Union decided that Bartholdi's statue would be presented as a gift from the people of France to the citizens of American. The financing of the monument would be split between the two countries. France would fund and build the statue itself, and America would be responsible for its pedestal.

Mr. Bartholdi presented his completed design to the Franco-American Union for approval. A vote was held, and the design was accepted by the members.

Now the fundraising could officially begin. The Franco-America Union devoted themselves to raising money to fund the statue.

CONSTRUCTION BEGINS

★ ★ ★

Certain that the money would soon be raised, Bartholdi began making models of his statue. He created several models, each larger than the last, until the desired dimensions were reached. This process kept the measurements precise. Such large-scale art required careful attention to detail and complete accuracy.

To begin, he constructed a 4½-foot (1.25 m) plaster model. This prototype of the statue was unveiled at the Paris dinner party held in 1865. Carefully doubling the measurements, a new plaster model was cast, now just over 9 feet (2.85 m) tall. These measurements were now tripled, and a third plaster model was made which measured 36 feet (11 m) tall.

Plaster model of the Statue of Liberty. Public domain.

As the plaster models became larger, the men realized the statue would not fit inside their Paris workshop. Devising an innovative solution, the 36-foot plaster model was carefully cut into eight sections. Then each individual section was enlarged to the desired size.

Wood frame and plaster molds.
Image credit: Albert Fernique, public domain.

Once each section of the plaster model was the correct size, a wooden mold was built to fit snugly inside it. This entire process required precision and accuracy. Any variance and the parts would not fit once pieced together. When each wooden frame was complete, the plaster cast was removed. The statue was now ready for her "skin."

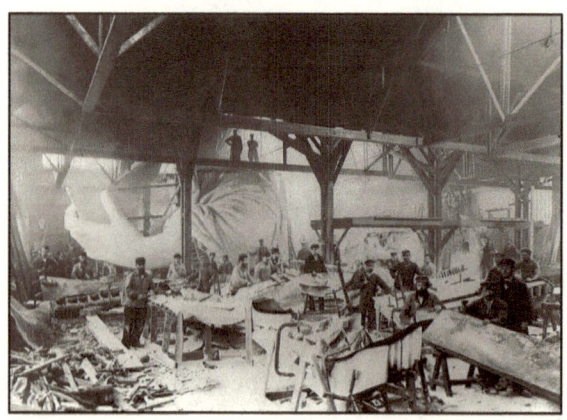

Workshop in Paris. Photo credit Albert Fernique, 1884. Public domain.

The statue was constructed in the 3000-square foot (278 m²) workshop which belonged to the architecture firm Gaget, Gauthier and Company. The workshop consisted of three separate buildings located at Numbers 21, 23, and 25 Rue de Chazelles. Building 21 held Frederic Bartholdi's personal office space. Number 23 Rue de Chazelles was where the plaster models were made and enlarged. Number 23 also held the metal forge which heated the copper plates in preparation for hammering. This site is also where Gustave Eiffel's team created the interior metal frame.

A PRETTY, YET PRACTICAL EXTERIOR

★ ★ ★

Mr. Bartholdi consulted with builders, artisans, and sculptors for the best material to cover his monument. The product must be strong, yet flexible, and able to withstand harsh weather conditions.

Marble, bronze, and copper were commonly used for statues. Marble and bronze posed two problems for Bartholdi's work: too heavy and too expensive. A decision was made that copper would be the best choice. Copper was lightweight yet sturdy and could withstand the wind and other elements. The element was also flexible and able to be shaped around the wood molds. As a bonus, after prolonged exposure to the salty air of New York Bay, the copper would age to an attractive blue-green patina, called verdigris. The Statue's current green color began to appear in the early 1900s.

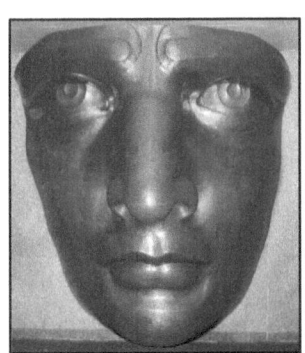 

Images: public domain.

French industrialist and art collector, Eugene Sebatan, generously donated 64 sheets (total weight 132,277 lbs/60,000 kilograms) of copper for the outer skin of the statue. His gift enabled work on the exterior to begin.

Mr. Bartholdi hired his workshop hosts, Gaget, Gauthier and Company to do the copper work. Mr. Gaget was an architect and Mr. Gauthier an engineer. They used an ancient metal-working technique called *repoussé* (meaning "push back") to shape the copper around the wooden frames.

Fitting the copper sheets to the wooden molds. Paris, France.
Image credit Albert Fernique, public domain.

The copper sheets were cut to the desired size, then heated in ovens to make them pliable. The men used hammers to beat the heated copper against the wood frame, to create the outer shape of the statue, called its "skin." Blowtorches were used to keep the metal soft while hammering. The copper was hammered to a thickness of $3/32^{nd}$ of an inch (22 mm) or approximately 2 pennies thick.

In all, 300 sheets of copper were used to create the outer skin of the enormous statue. During the initial assembly in Paris, the copper was secured to the frame with temporary screws, which enabled its quick and easy disassembly. Upon its assembly in America, the statue's outer shell was permanently secured to the iron frame, using about 300,000 copper rivets.

Copper panels inside the statue's skirt. Public domain.

Copper

American pennies dated prior to 1982 sometimes have a bluish-green discoloration due to a natural process called oxidation. When copper is exposed to air, its original dark orange pigment transforms into a bluish-green color. This color is called *patina*.

The value of copper has increased over the years. Due to its expense, the metal is no longer the main material used to mint pennies. Instead, today's American pennies are composed mostly of zinc.

Copper continues to be used for a variety of purposes. The metal is used in construction materials, such as wiring and plumbing. Copper is low-maintenance, corrosion-resistant and an excellent conductor of heat and electricity. Copper gutters and roofs are both durable and visually appealing. Common household cooking utensils such as pots and pans often contain copper as well.

THE STATUE'S INTERIOR

★ ★ ★

Once the exterior had been decided, Mr. Bartholdi turned his attention to the statue's inner framework. Like the statue's exterior, the structure had to be strong and durable, yet flexible enough to withstand high winds, as well as be inexpensive and portable.

Frédéric Bartholdi requested the advice of many structural engineers about the frame. From among these applicants, he chose French architect Eugène Viollet-le-Duc to design the statue's frame, or skeleton. Prior to working on the Statue of Liberty, Mr. Viollet-le-Duc had done restorative work on medieval buildings including the Cathedral Notre-Dame de Paris. Sadly, Eugène Viollet-le-Duc died suddenly in 1879 with the statue's skeleton only partially completed.

Image source: Manhhai, Flikr Creative Commons.

After Viollet-le-Duc's death, French civil engineer Alexandre Gustave Eiffel was hired to complete the statue's internal framework. Gustave Eiffel had built bridges and an innovative movable dome for the observatory in Nice, France. He began work on the statue in 1881.

As the Gaget and Gauthier team worked inside hammering the skin onto the wooden frames, Eiffel and his team worked on the supporting tower. Rejecting Viollet-le-Duc's plans for a single brick pier, Mr. Eiffel decided to use metal instead. He constructed four huge columns made of iron. These columns would support the statue's heavy outer framework of smaller metal bars. The copper skin would be attached using these bars.

The statue's huge frame was built on the ground, just outside Gaget and Gauthier's Paris workshop. When completed, the statue's frame contained 120 tons of wrought iron.

Inside view, showing the spiral stairs and steel supports. Image: NPS.

The predominantly hollow interior of the Statue of Liberty contains a support pylon holding a spiral staircase installed in its center. Four outer columns are connected to the center pylon with nine iron crossbars. The staircase allows visitors to climb the twenty stories to the statue's crown. Those who brave the strenuous climb are rewarded with a magnificent view.

Inside the crown. Image: NPS, public domain.

View from the crown. Photo credit, NPS CC SA 3.0 license.

When the statue was initially built, visitors could also climb a ladder placed inside the arm. This ladder led up to the torch's observation deck. This area has been permanently closed to the public.

Over 300 men were employed by Gaget, Gauthier and Company. These men worked around the clock to complete the statue. Several setbacks, including a lack of skilled laborers prolonged the build. In 1876 the plaster cast of a hand broke, forcing it to be remade.

Eiffel Tower

Several years after completing the Statue of Liberty, Gustave Eiffel built the Eiffel Tower. The project took two years to complete and was finished in time for the Paris Universal World Exposition of 1889.

This famous Paris landmark was not well received by onlookers who deemed it an ugly and useless eyesore. Only after the structure became a tourist attraction was the tower accepted as a work of art by the French.

Despite his many projects, including bridges, viaducts, and exposition buildings, Gustave Eiffel is best remembered for the tower that bears his name.

The Eiffel Tower in Paris, France.
Photo credit- Behn Lieu Song, used under
Wikimedia commons CC SA 3.0 license.

SHARING THE COST; THE FUNDRAISING BEGINS

★★★

Despite Mr. Secretan's generous donation of copper, much more money was needed to complete both the statue and its pedestal.

The Franco-American Union hosted its first fundraiser on November 6, 1875. A gala was held at the Hotel le Louvre in Paris. Two hundred guests were in attendance for the official unveiling of the plaster model. On display for the first time, Bartholdi's idea was finally tangible. Excitement grew and donations began to come in.

This banquet in Paris raised 40,000 francs, about 20 percent of the estimated cost. With these funds and the donated copper sheets, Frédéric Bartholdi was able to build the statue's head, arm, and torch the following year.

Not all fundraising efforts were successful, however. A special performance of composer Charles Gounod's hymn *Liberty Enlightening the World* held at the Paris Opera in 1876 was a flop.

As fundraising slowed, Bartholdi became discouraged. He briefly considered abandoning his project. Instead he soldiered on, selling pictures and postcards. He hired a French photographer, Albert Fernique, to take photos while the statue was being built.

Mr. Bartholdi charged admission to visitors at the Paris workshop where the statue was being built. Hundreds of people came by daily to view its progress. They were amazed by the statue's immense size. She was truly a remarkable sight. All funds raised were donated to the Statue's building project and used for laborers, materials, and tools.

Once completed, *Liberty Enlightening the World* stood 151 feet tall (46 meters) from her base to the torch. She towered above the Paris skyline.

The statue won the hearts of the Parisian people, who were reluctant to let her go. Several years later, a group of Americans living in France presented the people of Paris a replica of the Statue of Liberty. In place on the Isle of Swans, she stands 37 feet, 9 inches tall (11.5 m), facing her sister in America. In total, Paris has three replicas of Liberty Enlightening the World, including one sculpted by Mr. Bartholdi himself.

Assembly outside the Paris workshop.
Image source: public domain.

LIBERTY ON DISPLAY IN AMERICA

★★★

Remembering the excitement which the four-foot plaster model had received at its initial unveiling in 1875, Bartholdi and the French fundraisers devised a plan. They decided to create the most interesting parts of the statue first. These pieces would be placed on public display and used to generate both interest and financial support. The money raised would be used to finish building the remainder of the statue. The arm holding the torch was completed first. Its destination: Philadelphia.

The Centennial International Exposition, which was planned for 1876, would be held in Philadelphia's Fairmount Park from May 10–November 10. Here, Frédéric Bartholdi planned to introduce Lady Liberty to the American people and the world. However, much to Mr. Bartholdi's dismay, the hand and torch were not completed in time for the exposition's opening ceremony. He set sail for America in May 1876—alone.

Back in Paris, the work on Lady Liberty continued seven days per week. Soon the hand and torch were complete and shipped to Philadelphia. The pieces arrived in August of 1876. Measuring 30 feet (9 meters) tall, the display was quite impressive. Inside was a 42-foot (12.8 m) ladder which led to a small balcony around the torch. Standing on this ledge gave visitors a clear view of the surrounding area. As was hoped, people lined up to pay the 50 cents which allowed them to enjoy the view themselves.

Finally, the people of America could see and touch this amazing piece of art. Word soon began to spread about Bartholdi's enormous statue.

Torch on display at the 1876 Centennial Exposition in Philadelphia, PA. Image from Wikimedia commons, public domain.

During this Centennial Exposition, Frédéric Bartholdi met with Richard Morris Hunt, a successful American architect. Mr. Hunt had designed and built the Exposition's main exhibition hall. Impressed by this building, Mr. Bartholdi hired him to construct the pedestal upon which the statue would rest. Mr. Hunt had been educated in France and had adopted the French architectural style. His design was certain to complement the Statue's design.

Hunt had already designed the Tribune Building and the addition to the U.S. Capitol Building in Washington, D.C. Several years later he designed homes for rich and famous Americans, including J. J. Astor, George Vanderbilt's Biltmore House, and Cornelius Vanderbilt's summer home, The Breakers. Richard Hunt was a member of the Union League, the same anti-slavery group to which Laboulaye and Bartholdi belonged.

The Breakers, designed by Richard Morris Hunt. Image: public domain.

When the World's Fair ended in November 1876, the torch and arm were relocated to Madison Square Park in New York City. While the rest of the statue was being completed in Paris, the statue's portion remained here until 1882.

After the successful introduction of the hand and torch in America, the fundraisers decided to give the people of France a similar experience. The statue's head and crown were placed on display at the Paris Universal Exposition in 1878. A sign introduced her as *La Liberté Éclairant le Monde.* Two small replicas of the completed statue were placed on either side of the head, giving visitors a glimpse into the future. A donation to the statue's building fund allowed a person to climb a ladder up into the inside of the head and peer out of the crown's twenty-five windows.

In addition to this experience, pictures, postcards, and even a slideshow were available for purchase. Soon enough francs had been raised to pay for the statue in full. The total amount raised was ₣2,250,000 ($250,000 US).

*Head and crown on display 1878 in Paris, France.
Image credit: Albert Fernique, public domain.*

1876 Centennial Exposition In Philadelphia

The United States was given the privilege of hosting the 1876 World's Fair, also called the Centennial Exposition, which would be held in Philadelphia, Pennsylvania. In this city the Declaration of Independence had been signed 100 years earlier.

Thirty-eight countries and twenty colonies were represented at the Centennial Exposition. Part of this fair's purpose was to showcase America's industrial strength, skill, and innovation to the world. Some of the items featured included Mr. Alexander Graham Bell's telephone, Edison's phonograph, Samuel Colt's repeating revolver, a typewriter, and a calculator. New foods such as Heinz Tomato Ketchup™, popcorn, and Hires Root Beer™ were also showcased. Interesting to note, the Statue of Liberty was not the fair's main attraction. The Corliss Duplex Engine, able to power 800 machines at once, stole the show.

The fair featured a woman's pavilion with than 80 machines patented by female inventors. Inventions such as the dishwasher and self-heating iron had been designed to make their lives easier. The women's inventions were not accepted in the main exhibition buildings. Coordinated by Benjamin Franklin's great-granddaughter, Elizabeth Gillespie, the women financed and operated their pavilion independently.

Public attendance at the fair dwindled during the heat of the summer, but in the fall these numbers improved. By November, the Centennial Exposition was declared a success. Over eight million visitors had attended the fair.

As a result of the World's Fair, public perception of the United States changed. America became recognized worldwide as a competitor in innovation and industrialization. The demand for American-made products increased internationally.

Memorial Hall, built for the Centennial Exposition in Philadelphia, 1876.
Image: public domain.

PERMISSION GRANTED

Years prior, upon returning from his trip abroad in 1870, Mr. Bartholdi wrote to President Ulysses S. Grant. He requested permission to use Bedloe's Island as the statue's permanent home. Several years passed before he received an answer. During this time, President Rutherford B. Hayes assigned General W. T. Sherman the task of selecting an appropriate site for France's proposed gift.

Honoring Bartholdi's wishes, General Sherman agreed to make Bedloe's Island the Statue of Liberty's permanent home. Congress voted in favor of this proposal in 1877. Lady Liberty had found her new home.

FUNDRAISING IN AMERICA

While France had successfully raised all the funds necessary to build the statue by the year 1880, across the Atlantic progress proceeded slowly. Both the U.S. Congress and New York's governor had refused to fund the pedestal. Raising the money was dependent on private citizens.

In general, the American people were not excited about the monument. In fact, many influential businessmen and leaders initially opposed the idea. Some believed only American-made art should be displayed. Others believed the statue cost too much money and would be too much trouble to maintain. The *New York Times* declared the statue "wasteful and useless." A statue celebrating freedom was unnecessary to these Americans.

Aware that Boston and Philadelphia had shown interest in the statue, Mr. Bartholdi saw an opportunity. He started a rumor with a tease: if New York City didn't want the statue, perhaps another city might. Apprehensive about losing the statue, New Yorkers began to show a greater interest in her. Bartholdi's ploy had worked successfully. Once again donations began to trickle in.

In 1877 an official pedestal fundraising committee, the American Committee of the Statue of Liberty was formed. One of their first campaigns involved selling tiny replicas of the statue. A six-inch (15 cm) model sold for one dollar, while one which stood twelve inches tall (30 cm) sold for five dollars. Other fundraising efforts included prizefights and theatrical performances.

The artistic community rallied behind the statue's fundraising. Writers, including Mark Twain and Walt Whitman, donated poems and short stories to be sold at auction. The *Bartholdi Pedestal Fund Art Exhibition* displayed these literary works prior to the auction. The art show was held in Brooklyn, New York over a three-week period in January 1884.

Art Exhibit Poster for pedestal fundraiser.
Source: NYPL digital collection, public domain.

At this exhibition the now-famous poem by Emma Lazarus was first read. She had composed her sonnet titled *The New Colossus* at the urging of the event's organizer, Constance Cary Harrison. Initially reluctant to participate, Miss Lazarus eventually agreed. She wrote the poem in two days. Her sonnet sold for $1,500 USD (about $37,000 today). The poem was later included in a souvenir pamphlet published by Constance Cary Harrison. This publication featured writings from the literary talent who had donated to the statue's art exhibition.

The New Colossus by Emma Lazarus. Image - Library of Congress 1883, public domain.

THE PEDESTAL
★★★

In 1882 American engineer Richard Morris Hunt began to design the pedestal. After requesting many revisions of Mr. Hunt's sketches, Frédéric Bartholdi gave his approval. The final design, which was grand but modest and not ornamental, directs the viewer's attention not upon the pedestal itself, but toward the statue.

When work on the pedestal was begun, about $145,000 USD had been raised. Roughly $100,000 USD more was needed to complete the project.

Budget constraints played a key role in the pedestal's design. Originally planned to total 117 feet (35.6 m), the builders settled on a tower which would stand 89 feet (27 m) tall. Though Mr. Hunt initially proposed a pedestal made of solid granite, he was forced to settle for a less expensive option. Granite stone blocks would cover poured concrete walls.

Excavation of the pedestal's foundation began in April 1883. Part of Fort Wood's appeal was its 24-foot-high walls. This existing star-shaped structure was used as the basis for the pedestal's foundation. However, excavating the old fort proved to be more difficult than the men had hoped. The fortress contained solid concrete bomb shelters, and the concrete had to be broken into pieces and painstakingly removed.

Once the debris was cleared away, a 20-foot (6 m) pit was excavated inside the star-shaped walls. Fresh concrete was poured into the huge hole, creating a solid foundation upon which to build the pedestal. The pedestal was constructed in three tiers. Fifty feet (15 m) from the top of the pedestal, four iron beams were set vertically into the concrete. These beams would attach to the statue's four metal supports.

Building the pedestal. Image source: public domain.

Once the concrete inner portion had been completed, the pedestal's face (the outer, visible portion) was covered with decorative granite stone blocks. The granite was transported to New York from Connecticut. The *John Beattie Granite Works* company supplied the granite slabs used for the pedestal's decorative outer layer.

Inside the pedestal a staircase was built, totaling 215 steps from the ground floor to the top. An observation platform for visitors was placed at the foot of the statue. An elevator was also added, making the small balcony accessible to all.

The pedestal's cornerstone was laid in a Masonic ceremony on August 5, 1884. Braving the pouring rain, about 1,500 people attended the ceremony. A copper time capsule was placed into a small hole underneath the cornerstone. Inside the capsule was a copy of the Declaration of Independence, a copy of the U.S. Constitution, several medals, a list of the Masonic Grand Lodge Masters of New York, a newspaper, and several other articles deemed appropriate.

The pedestal's cornerstone. Image: public domain.

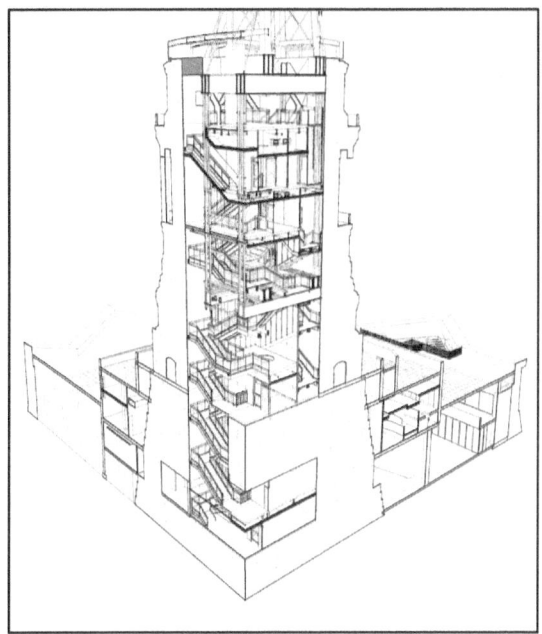

Map of the pedestal.

PULITZER'S CROWDFUNDING CAMPAIGN

★ ★ ★

Work on the pedestal continued steadily for a total of eighteen months, until December 1884, when the money ran out. Unable to pay for workers or materials, construction came to a complete halt. A new fundraising effort was needed.

Publisher Joseph Pulitzer had participated in the pedestal's fundraising efforts before. He had placed advertisements in his newspaper *New York World* to promote the sale of souvenirs. In March 1885 he launched a new campaign.

He wrote an editorial about the Statue of Liberty and placed it on the front page of his newspaper. He wrote about how the people of France had supported giving the significant gift to America. Many working-class French citizens had donated their hard-earned money to fund the project. Mr. Pulitzer encouraged Americans of all status and ability to donate toward the pedestal's completion. For a donation of any amount, he promised to publish the donor's name in *New York World*.

His efforts paid off. Donations rolled in—from school children, manual laborers, newly arrived immigrants, and businessmen alike. Gifts of every amount, some merely pennies, counted toward the goal. Mr. Pulitzer made good on his promise and lists of the donors' names appeared in the *New York World*. At times he published personal notes sent to him by the donors. A successful campaign indeed, in just over five months (by August 1885), American citizens had given $101,091 toward the pedestal fund.

The unexpected benefit of this crowdfunding campaign was now the American people felt connected to and vested in the Statue of Liberty. They had played a part in its creation, which left them with a feeling of pride and importance. The American citizens had now accepted the statue and had adopted her into their hearts. Then the Statue of Liberty truly became a gift from the people of France to the people of America—not only the wealthy and powerful, but ordinary citizens as well.

August 11, 1885- front page of The World newspaper.
Image source: Wikimedia, public domain.

A Gift For Frederic Bartholdi

Joseph Pulitzer's fundraising efforts resulted in a surplus of money. These excess funds were used to provide Mr. Bartholdi with a gift from the American people. The jewelry boutique, Tiffany's, designed the gift—a silver globe topped with a replica of the statue's torch and hand.

ASSEMBLY IN FRANCE

★ ★ ★

Back in France, the statue, which had been assembled for quite some time, was ready. Lady Liberty waited patiently for her base to be completed.

In 1884 the statue's head, torch, and arm had been returned to the Paris workshop. When all the statue's parts were finally together, Lady Liberty was erected in the courtyard outside the Paris workshop of Gaget, Gauthier and Company. The workers stood on a complex frame of scaffolding built around the statue while assembling her many parts. Once completed, she stood proudly in France for nearly a year while the pedestal was completed in New York. The people of France, who had fallen in love with her, were reluctant to let her go.

France officially gave the gift to America in a ceremony held on July 4, 1884. The Franco-American Union led by Ferdinand, Viscount de Lesseps presented the Statue to the citizens of the United States. The American Foreign Minister to France, Levi P. Morton accepted the gift on behalf of the American people. The French Prime Minister, Jules Ferry, was ill and unable to attend.

Outside the workshop in Paris.
Image: Wikimedia commons, public domain.

THE PEDESTAL IS COMPLETE

★ ★ ★

Once the funding was secured, work on the pedestal resumed. As it neared completion, several coins were tossed into the concrete foundation, commemorating the donors who had made the pedestal possible. The pedestal was finished nearly one year later, on April 22, 1886. It had taken three years to construct.

Richard Morris Hunt received $1,000 for his design. He generously donated this money to the pedestal's American fundraising committee.

A NEW HOME
★ ★ ★

In the early spring of 1885, the statue was prepared for her trip across the Atlantic. The pedestal had not yet been completed, but the men remained hopeful that it would be soon.

To prepare for her journey, the statue was dismantled into 305 parts. These parts were carefully labeled to make reconstructing her in America easier and more efficient. The pieces were placed into 214 crates which were then loaded onto seventeen train cars. The statue was transported by rail to the port city of Rouen, France. Upon the ship's arrival in Rouen, the crates were loaded onto the French warship, *Isere*.

The *Isere* set sail on April 21, 1885. The trip across the Atlantic was not uneventful. The ship encountered a storm, then ran out of coal to power her steam engines. The *Isere* relied on her sails for the remainder of the journey, causing a delay in her arrival. A trip that normally took 2 weeks to reach the destination, the *Isere* needed 27 days. This delay was not terribly problematic as the pedestal had not yet been completed.

Thousands of people gathered to greet the *Isere* as the warship sailed into New York Bay. The ship paused briefly before reaching her destination so that its cargo—the statue—could be signed over to General Charles P. Stone, the statue's American engineer. The *Isere* docked at Bedloe's Island on June 17, 1885.

Unloading the heavy crates containing the statue required several days of backbreaking work. After they had been unloaded, one problem remained. The pedestal was still incomplete. Unable to begin assembling the statue, the crates were placed in storage.

Unloading the crates from the Isere, 1885.
Image: NPS, public domain.

On November 4, 1885, Frédéric Bartholdi arrived to oversee the reconstruction of his statue, he did not expect such a long wait. Finally, in April 1886, nearly a year after her arrival in America, *Liberty Enlightening the World* was unboxed. Her many parts were pieced together like a puzzle. During the statue's assembly the workers discovered that some parts had been mislabeled. This unexpected inconvenience took some time to resolve.

Hundreds of workers, many of them recent immigrants, worked to reconstruct the statue. To decrease travel expenses and save time, these workers were housed on the island.

They began the process by building the statue's metal frame and securing the four columns to the pedestal's iron beams. Next came the outer shell. Steam-powered cranes hoisted the materials into place. The carefully shaped copper plates were attached in such a way as to allow movement in high winds, as well as with temperature changes. In all, over 300,000 copper rivets attached the "skin" to it iron frame.

Reconstructing the statue's iron frame.
Image: public domain.

The assembly work was dangerous. The statue's base was too narrow to build a scaffold. Instead, the men were forced to dangle from ropes as they worked. Mercifully, no one lost his life.

Lady Liberty's face, which was the final part to be assembled, remained covered until the presentation ceremony in October. The entire reconstruction had taken four months.

Above: The statue's feet and the torch base.

The statue's face. Images: public domain.

The Isere

Commissioned in 1866 to active service in the French navy, the *Isere* measured 227 feet long (69.2 m) and 31 feet (9.43 m) wide. She was built with a strong metal hull and used to haul heavy military supplies. Equipped to travel long distances, she had two means of propulsion: a 160-horsepower coal-fired steam engine and three masts with sails.

Heavily damaged during the Second World War, her wreckage lies off the coast of St. Catherine in Locmiquelic.

Isere's captain, Gabriel Lespinasse de Sauline was 39 years old when he guided the Statue of Liberty across the Atlantic.

LIBERTY ENLIGHTENING THE WORLD

Finally, after 21 years of planning, fundraising, and construction, *Liberty Enlightening the World* was home. She was officially presented to the American people by the citizens of France on October 28, 1886.

More than one million people gathered in lower Manhattan to celebrate this momentous occasion. The entire city was shut down. Schools and businesses were closed, and people came from all over to view the ceremony.

Though the air was gray with fog and the sky threatened rain, it could not dampen the excitement in New York City. A celebratory parade was held. The Statue engineer, General Charles P. Stone, was the parade's grand marshal. Thousands of people participated in the event, including several Masonic Lodges.

Marching from Fifth Avenue and Broadway to the Battery situated at the tip of Manhattan, the parade detoured to pass the front of the *New York World* office. As it passed the New York Stock Exchange, the traders threw streams of ticker tape paper into the crowds.

Eager onlookers waved French and American flags as they stood by the street or peered out of open windows. Banners of red, white, and blue lined the parade route.

That afternoon, the President's yacht, the *Despatch* carried 600 people to Bedloe's Island for the unveiling. Onboard the yacht were international dignitaries and those responsible for the Statue's construction.

As the ship approached Bedloe's Island, the rain began and continued throughout the day and into the night. Fireworks had been planned for the evening but were postponed due to the dismal weather.

Anxious to be a part of this momentous occasion, many onlookers chartered boats, crowding the harbor. Dark smoke billowed from the many steamships idling in the Bay. Pedestrians who had gathered at the Battery strained to watch the proceedings across the water. Their view of the Statue was obscured by the thick smoke, rainy mist, and dark clouds.

October 28, 1886. Image: NPS, public domain.

On Bedloe's Island the ceremony began. Approximately 2,500 people had been invited to witness this event. President Grover Cleveland had the honor of fastening the statue's final rivet.

During the celebratory speeches, Auguste Bartholdi slipped away and climbed inside the statue to the torch. High above the crowds, he watched the proceedings from the torch's balcony. In his hand he held a rope that had been secured to a large flag draped over the statue's face. Misreading his cue, Mr. Bartholdi prematurely pulled the rope, releasing the French flag.

Lady Liberty's unveiling was greeted by enthusiastic applause. A full 15 minutes lapsed before President Cleveland could begin his speech. In conclusion, he stated, "Liberty's light shall pierce the darkness of ignorance and men's oppression until liberty shall enlighten the world."

Emma Lazarus's poem, *The New Colossus,* was not read that day; in fact, it was not mentioned at all. Also absent were Édouard Laboulaye and Gustave Eiffel. Mr. Laboulaye had died in 1883, and Mr. Eiffel was in France, busy working on another project.

★★★
Ticker Tape Parades

Narrow, one-inch-wide paper was used in machines called "tickers," to print stock quotes. During the October 28, 1886, parades, enthusiastic stockbrokers joined in the festivity by tossing ribbons of ticker paper out their office windows onto the streets below.

This event marked the beginning of a tradition that has become a hallmark of New York City celebrations. Though the first ticker-tape parade was spontaneous, they are now carefully planned. New York City's mayor decides who receives the honor of a ticker-tape parade.

NYC Tickertape parade for Gordon Cooper, 1963.
Image: NASA, public domain.

FRIENDSHIP AND FREEDOM | 71

Notable ticker tape parades include:
- In 1910, greeting former President Teddy Roosevelt's return from an expedition in Africa
- In 1927, celebrating Charles Lindberg's successful solo flight across the Atlantic
- In 1962, celebrating the New York Mets' first game as a member of the National League

Ticker-tape is no longer used on Wall Street or for the parades. It has been replaced with shredded paper and confetti.

LIGHTING THE TORCH
★★★

One of the most anticipated events that day was the illumination of the torch. Unfortunately, the heavy rain caused both the torch lighting and the planned fireworks display to be postponed. Several days later, on November 1, the clear night skies finally allowed the gathered crowds to enjoy the elaborate fireworks display.

The torch's long-awaited lighting on the first of November proved to be anti-climactic. Once lit, the torch cast a dark shadow on the Statue of Liberty's face and shoulders. The angle of the light had been miscalculated; her face could not be seen. Several adjustments were needed before the lighting issue was figured out. The use of electrical lamps was new at this time, and the engineers were still unfamiliar with the technology.

The Army Corps of Engineers, who had ordered a last-minute change to the torch's design, were partly to blame for this mishap. Bartholdi's' plans called for floodlights to be placed on the torch's balcony. The Army Engineers feared that the floodlights would be too bright for passing ships. Bartholdi was given one week to change the lighting design. He moved the lamps inside the torch, cutting several windows in the copper for the light to pass through.

The American Electric Manufacturing Company had generously donated the nine lamps and other lighting equipment for the statue's torch. The company also agreed to fund the lights for one week, until other means could be found to cover the expense. By the time the lamps were properly adjusted, the promised week was over. Government officials begged the American Electric Manufacturing Company for one more night so Mr. Bartholdi could see his statue properly lit. The company agreed. Impressed with the statue and satisfied with the lighting, Mr. Bartholdi sailed home to France. The torch, however, remained dark for two weeks while its funding was debated. Eventually President Cleveland authorized the Lighthouse Board to fund the torch and its care.

Designed as a lighthouse, the torch was expected to be visible for 50 miles out to sea. Ironically, the modified torch was now too dim and only visible for 24 miles. The holes which had been cut into the shell still did not allow enough light to pass through.

The Statue of Liberty functioned as a working lighthouse for five years. Its keeper, Albert E. Littlefield, was paid $1,000 per year. Mr. Littlefield, his family, and his assistants lived in a small home on the island.

A problem since the beginning, the torch lights have been replaced and improved several times. Today a combination of bulbs inside the torch provide light roughly equivalent to 2,500 times the brilliance of the moon.

CONTROVERSY

At least three distinct groups of people did not join in the festivities held October 28, 1886. The freedoms which the statue proclaimed were lacking in their daily lives. In fact, they saw the statue as a slap in the face.

Women suffragists noted that among the 2500 invited guests on Bedloe's Island only two were female- and one was a child. To these women, the statue was a parody. They found it ironic that this icon to freedom was female at a time when American women did not enjoy the same freedoms as American men, including the right to vote. The women, members of the New York State Women's Suffrage Association, chartered their own boat from which to protest the statue's dedication.

Also absent among the invited guests were people of color, most notably African Americans and Chinese immigrants. Though the statue was created to celebrate the end of slavery in America, these freed slaves were not accepted as equals. Their exclusion at the statue's unveiling was another reminder of the injustice they endured. Though the Emancipation Proclamation Act of 1863 declared them free, they continued to be treated unfairly. In fact, laws had been written to reduce their rights as citizens. They were refused job opportunities, sufficient pay, housing, and proper education.

Approximately one month after the statue's unveiling, an ad was placed in the *Cleveland Gazette* by an African American man. In it, he condemned the unfair treatment of the black community. The ad urged that the statue be pushed into the harbor "until all are treated equal."

The third group unhappy with the statue were the workers. Working conditions were harsh, and pay was extremely poor. Wages had plummeted in recent years as new immigrants arrived, all willing to work for less money. Dependent on their employers, yet desiring better working conditions, these laborers organized rallies to object to their mistreatment. In 1882 when the first Labor Day was held, more than 10,000 New York City workers marched in protest.

In fact, in 1886 this ideal of freedom in America was mainly enjoyed by the wealthy. These rich Americans enjoyed lavish lifestyles and surrounded themselves with others in similar circumstances. Secure in their elitist circles, they were disconnected from the plight of immigrants and unaffected by the harsh realities faced by the poor. They were content to live in a protective bubble.

SYMBOLISM
★ ★ ★

The Statue of Liberty was given to Americans as a sign of friendship between two allied nations and to celebrate the end of slavery. Over the years, with the help of Emma Lazarus's poem, the statue has grown to become a well-known symbol of inspiration, hope, and strength through adversity.

An examination of her individual parts reveals ideals, or beliefs, that the sculptor, Frédéric Bartholdi, thought were important.

Her diadem (crown) has seven points, or rays. The number seven represents both the seven continents and the seven seas. The pointed rays signify light, suggesting the idea that the United States offers the light of liberty to the world.

The Statue's left arm holds a tablet, which is symbolic of a nation governed by law. This tablet is a *tabula ansata*, which is Latin for "tablet with handles," a popular design in ancient Rome. The tablet reads July IV MDCCLXXVI, the date the Declaration of Independence was signed (July 4, 1776).

Held in her right hand, the torch is a symbol of enlightenment. With it, she lights the path to freedom and liberty.

Under her feet lie broken chains; her right foot is lifted as if to step forward. She steps out of the chains of oppression and tyranny into a new life of freedom.

Images NPS, public domain.

Even the statue's pedestal itself has symbolic references. Its granite face has thirteen layers, one for each of the original colonies.

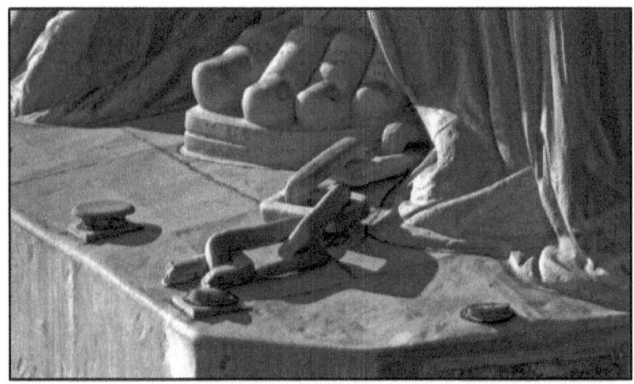

Image: NPS, public domain.

THE POEM

Today thinking of the Statue of Liberty without remembering the phrase, "Give me your tired, your poor, your huddled masses…" is difficult. These words, written by poet Emma Lazarus propelled the Statue of Liberty into a symbol of hope and rebirth—not only for Americans, but worldwide. Written in two days by a reluctant Emma Lazarus, this poem was never intended to be displayed on the statue itself. In fact, it was almost not written at all.

As a young Jewish woman, Emma had composed many poems dedicated to injustice. She used her fame to shine light on the harsh lives of poor immigrants, especially her people—the Jews. Forced to flee Russia to avoid religious persecution, these Jewish immigrants were held on Ward's Island while government officials processed their documents. Living in crowded and unsanitary conditions, they anxiously awaited their fate.

When asked to contribute a poem to the art exhibition, Emma was reluctant. She did not want any distractions from her work with the immigrants. Only the words of her friend and fellow poet, Constance Cary Harrison, convinced her to compose a poem for the auction. Mrs. Harrison encouraged Emma to imagine the statue was holding her torch out toward the Jewish refugees for whom Emma usually wrote and dedicated her poems.

After the auction, Miss Lazarus's poem was all but forgotten. Nearly twenty years later, the poem was revitalized by a friend. In 1903 Emma Lazarus' poem, *The New Colossus* was inscribed on a plaque and displayed inside the pedestal. The words of this poem transformed the statue to a beacon of hope amidst suffering. Today, the Statue of Liberty holds high her torch with the same message of hope, welcoming all who bravely seek a better life.

Emma Lazarus's Poem is inscribed on a plaque originally displayed on the Statue of Liberty's pedestal. Photo: NPS, public domain.

MAINTENANCE AND RESTORATION

★ ★ ★

Caring for the Statue of Liberty is a huge responsibility and quite expensive. Over the years, the Statue of Liberty has undergone minor changes, multiple repairs, and a major restoration. The National Park Service, together with the Statue of Liberty - Ellis Island Foundation, oversee the fundraising which pays for the care and maintenance of the Statue. Donations are sought from citizens and private corporations.

1916

The Statue of Liberty's right arm and torch were severely damaged in 1916 when an ammunition storage facility exploded off the coast of New Jersey. This explosion, known as the Black Tom explosion, was an act of sabotage by German spies.

The blast also shattered several windows in the crown and blew off plates of copper and rivets. The statue was closed for two weeks to undergo repairs. Unfortunately, the damage to the statue's arm was so extensive that access to the torch was permanently closed to tourists.

Sculptor Gutzon Borglum, creator of Mount Rushmore, was hired to repair and renovate the torch. He cut additional holes in the torch and installed 250 pieces of custom-fit yellow glass. The pieces were held together by copper strips.

The 1930s

Extensive improvements and several repairs were made in preparation for the statue's fiftieth birthday. The National Park Service, which had taken over the island's care, used hundreds of laborers provided by the Public Works Administration. In an effort to enhance the visitor's experience, accessibility to the island was improved. Old buildings were demolished, a new dock was installed, and the sea wall was repaired. The areas surrounding the monument were landscaped and a new walkway was built. A new staircase was built in the pedestal, along with an enlarged public entrance.

In addition to her cosmetic changes, the Statue of Liberty underwent much-needed repairs. In 1937 those responsible for the maintenance of the statue discovered water seeping into the pedestal. A copper skirt, called flashing, was installed around the statue's base to prevent seawater and rain from leaking in. The pedestal also received a heating system and a new elevator.

The statue herself received attention. Each ray of the crown was removed, and the rusted interiors were repaired. The corroded cast-iron staircase leading to the crown was repaired. Much of the statue's interior paint was burned and scraped off, then a new coat applied. This paint was to slow the corrosion of the iron bars. The broken glass windows in the torch were replaced.

The 1980s

In the 1980s in preparation for Lady Liberty's one-hundredth birthday celebration, an $87 million dollar restoration was undertaken. Her copper skin was cleaned, her corroded metal was repaired, and the torch was completely replaced.

Structural engineers from America and France worked together to carefully examine the statue, determining the statue was severely corroded in several locations. Inside the statue, layers of old paint were removed and replaced with a zinc silicate primer called IC 531. The primer provided corrosion resistance. About 1,800 iron bars which secured the copper skin to the frame were replaced by Teflon-coated stainless-steel supports. The original iron bars are on display at the Statue of Liberty Museum which opened in May 2019.

During this renovation, engineers were surprised to discover that the statue's head was two feet off center, and its arm was misaligned by eighteen inches. The decision to repair rather than rebuild these misaligned portions was made. Additional supports were added inside these structures to preserve their integrity.

Workers inside the statue had to wear special suits equipped with a breathing apparatus. Under Bartholdi's direction, an asbestos-based substance had been applied to slow corrosion. This substance was removed and discovered to have been largely ineffective. Areas of the statue's copper skin had unrepairable holes. New copper skin coverings were molded and applied. These new skins were created from the roof of an old building with a green patina that closely resembled Lady Liberty's.

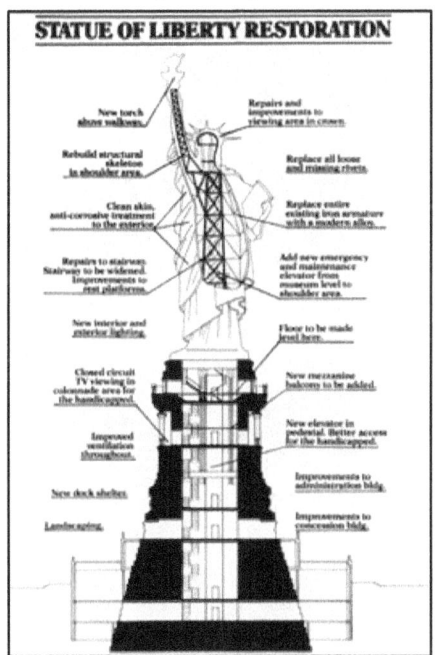

Diagram of restorative work done in the 1980's. Image: NPS.

The minimal number of photos that had been taken during the statue's original construction posed a problem for those working on the restoration. Learning from the past's mistakes, photographers were hired to document this renovation in great detail. This photographic evidence was carefully saved to assist in future renovations.

Maintenance workers determined the amber glass windows, which had been added to the torch in 1916, were leaking. As a result, the torch had suffered severe water damage to the flame and upper portion. Therefore, in 1985 the decision was made to replace rather than repair the torch due to the extensive water damage. The new torch was an exact replica of Bartholdi's original design, containing no windows. The flame is now covered in 24-carat gold. Reflecting the sun's rays during the day, the flame is lit by sixteen floodlights at night.

The original torch went on a worldwide tour before being installed as an exhibit in the pedestal lobby. It now permanently resides in the Statue of Liberty Museum, which opened in May 2019.

Image credit: Peter Arnott, CC SA license 3.0.

Other improvements addressed safety and making the visitors experience more enjoyable. A larger entrance and an elevator were installed in the pedestal, and lighting, heating and ventilation systems were improved. A tiny, three-person elevator was installed in the statue itself to quickly bring down people from the crown in case of an emergency. This elevator is also used by statue maintenance workers but is not open to the general public. Tourists' complaints, such as the ferry service and long lines to enter the crown, were addressed. A ticketing process was implemented, limiting the number of daily visitors to Bedloe's Island. A ticket was also required to enter the pedestal and the crown. As a result, wait times decreased.

★★★

Liberty Weekend July 1986

The centennial celebration (one-hundredth birthday) of the statue *Liberty Enlightening the World*. The celebration began on Thursday, the third of July with a boat parade and a church service. Speeches made by President Ronald Reagan and France's President François Mitterrand were televised around the world. A special citizenship ceremony to welcome new Americans was held on Ellis Island. That night the statue's new torch was lit for the first time by President Reagan.

The weekend's festivities included an airshow, concerts, parades, a triathlon, and a liberty-themed conference. Numerous food booths occupied lower Manhattan. On the Fourth of July, an impressive fireworks display lit up the night sky.

First Lady Nancy Reagan and Walter Cronkite officially reopened the Statue of Liberty monument on Saturday, July 5.

First Lady Nancy Reagan officially re-opened the crown July 5, 1986.
Photo credit: Bill Fitz-Patrick. Public domain.

The 2000s

The statue was closed for a year beginning October 29, 2011, for important safety upgrades and renovations. The fire suppression, electrical and mechanical systems received updates. A new code-compliant stairwell and elevator were installed, and visitor restrooms were rehabilitated.

Inside the statue a second spiral staircase was added. One set of stairs is now designated for walking up to the crown and the other for descending. Each staircase has 146 narrow steps. For those needing a break from climbing stairs, two rest platforms are provided with a walkway between. This also enables those who are unable to complete the climb to descend more easily.

The new spiral staircase inside the Statue of Liberty.
Image: public domain, Wikimedia commons.

Five web cameras were installed around the statue's torch. These cameras allow people an up close and personal view of the Statue of Liberty. Two cameras point inward toward the frame and the torch itself. Three outer cameras give viewers worldwide the opportunity to enjoy live views of the harbor and surrounding areas.

These cameras can be viewed online at:
- https://www.libertyellisfoundation.org/torchcam
- https://www.earthcam.net/projects/statueofliberty/ellisisland

In May 2019, the newly constructed, privately financed Statue of Liberty Museum opened. Three times the size of the original museum, which had been located in the pedestal's basement, this modern facility can easily accommodate the thousands of tourists who visit Liberty Island each day. Featuring several videos which recount the statue's history, the museum also contains the statue's original torch and a replica of the statue's face.

Statue of Liberty Museum, July 2019.
By Epicgenius -used under CC BY-SA 4.0, wikicommons.

CONCLUSION
★ ★ ★

The Statue of Liberty's story is one of collaboration, perseverance, and triumph over adversity. A true labor of love, she stands today as a tribute to her many designers, engineers, and caretakers. Beloved by Americans and admired worldwide, she has become one of the most recognized symbols of the United States.

STATUE OF LIBERTY FACTS

★ ★ ★

Total construction time from idea to completion: 21 years

Statue cost: ₣2,250,000 ($250,000 USD, which is about $5.4 million USD today)

Pedestal cost: $250,000 (about $5.4 million USD today)

Pedestal height: 154 feet (46.9 m)

Statue height from base to torch: 151 feet (46 m)

Statue height from heel to top of head: 111 feet 1 inch (33.8 m)

Total height: 305 feet (93 m)

Thickness of tablet: 2 feet (0.6 m)

Length of right arm: 42 feet (12.8 m)

Foot: 25 feet (7.6 m)

Nose: 4½ feet long (1.4 m)

Index Finger: 8 feet (2.4 m)

Width at waist: 35 feet (10.6 m)

Width of mouth: 3 feet (0.9 m)

Length of sandal: 25 feet (7.6 m)

Shoe size: 879

Number of stairs from foot to crown: 146

Number of stairs in pedestal: 215

Statue weight: 225 tons

THE PEOPLE BEHIND THE STATUE

Frédéric Auguste Bartholdi

Born: August 2, 1834, in Colmar, France

Died: October 4, 1904, in Paris, France, of tuberculosis at the age of 70.

Following his father's death, Frédéric's mother took him and his older brother, Jean, to live in Paris. Showing an early interest in drawing, he studied architecture and painting. One of his teachers was architect Eugène Emmanuel Viollet-le-Duc.

F. Bartholdi - wikicommons, public domain.

A trip to Egypt and Yemen in the 1850s with fellow artists sparked his interest in massive sculptures. A Freemason, he knew many influential members of French society.

Bartholdi is best known for two massive works: the Statue of Liberty and the Lion of Belfort. His childhood home in Colmar, France, opened to visitors as the Bartholdi Museum in 1922.

Alexandre-Gustave Eiffel

Born: December 15, 1832, in Dijon, France

Died: December 27, 1923 in Paris, France, of a stroke at age 91.

Alexandre- Gustave Eiffel, Wikimedia commons, public domain.

As a young man, Gustave Eiffel studied chemistry in hopes he would take over his uncle's vinegar factory. Failing to receive the inheritance, he studied metallurgy. Educated as a civil engineer, he began his career building bridges and railroad stations. Soon he shared his expertise internationally, building structures in Spain, Romania, and Mexico. Impressed with his work, Bartholdi hired Eiffel to complete the Statue of Liberty's skeleton after the sudden death of his initial engineer.

When France held a contest to design a tower for the 1889 World's Fair, Gustave's design was selected from 700 entrants. Though unpopular at first, the Eiffel Tower is now one of the most visited monuments worldwide. He was given the nickname "Magician of Iron."

Albert Fernique

Born: June 30, 1841, in Paris, France

Died: 1898 in Paris, France.

An engineer with a passion for photography, Fernique was well-known for photos of structures as well as his use of ambient light and photoengraving. Frédéric Bartholdi hired him to document the construction of the Statue of Liberty in Paris. Many of his photographs still exist and provide an invaluable record of the Statue's history.

A. Fernique and family c. 1875, photo from Wikimedia commons - public domain.

Richard Morris Hunt

Born: October 31, 1827, in Brattleboro, Vermont

Died: July 31, 1895, in Newport, Rhode Island of heart failure at the age of 67

Following his father's death, his mother moved the family to Europe. Richard studied art in Rome but was encouraged by his family to enroll in the École des Beaux-Arts, the finest architecture school in the world. He was the first American admitted. Frédéric Bartholdi attended this influential art school briefly.

Richard Morris Hunt, NPS.

He returned to the United States where one of his first projects was assisting in the renovation of the U.S. Capitol Building, in 1856. His extroverted personality won him wealthy clients.

Designing estates for America's rich and famous, his work includes the Biltmore Estate, Belcourt Castle, and the Tribune Building. He founded the American Institute of Architects and the Municipal Art Society. After his death, his son Richard took over his last project, a wing at the New York Metropolitan Museum of Art.

Édouard René Lefebvre de Laboulaye

Born: January 18, 1811, in Paris, France

Died: May 25, 1883, in Paris, France

The son of a wealthy family, Laboulaye received an excellent education. Graduating with a law degree, he became politically active and was an outspoken advocate for abolition.

An admirer of the United States, he was an expert on American politics and authored several books on the subject.

Married twice, his first marriage ended with his wife's premature death in 1841, when the couple's son, Paulin, was nine. He remarried and had two more sons, Antione, and Rene-Victor.

Source: Wikimedia commons, public domain.

Sadly, he did not live to see the statue completed, dying seven months before the statue was erected in Paris.

Emma Lazarus

Born: July 22, 1849, in New York, New York

Died: November 19, 1887, in New York of Hodgkin's lymphoma at the age of 37

The daughter of a wealthy sugar merchant, Emma Lazarus was well educated and indulged. She began to write poetry at the age of eleven. Her father saw her talent and paid to have her poems published. He ensured she was among influential people which helped to promote her to fame.

Emma Lazarus
Source: public domain.

Though rich, Emma cared deeply for others. The great-granddaughter of Jewish immigrants, she took a special interest in the plight of her people. She wrote essays, poems and articles defending persecuted Jews around the world.

She supported refugees who were forced to live in unsanitary and unacceptable conditions. She specifically supported those Jews who had been forced to flee religious persecution from Russia. Emma volunteered her time and talents, raising money and calling attention to the plight of these poor people.

Her poem, *The New Colossus,* was instrumental in associating the Statue of Liberty with immigration. In the poem, she addressed her belief that America needed to be a welcoming, safe haven for all.

Joseph Pulitzer

Born: April 10, 1847, in Mako, Hungary

Died: October 29, 1911, in Charleston, South Carolina

He immigrated to the United States as a recruit for the Union Army during the Civil War. After the war, he moved to St. Louis where he became a reporter for a German newspaper.

Active in politics, he was elected to the Missouri state legislature in 1869.

In 1878 he purchased two newspapers and merged them as the *St Louis Post-Dispatch*. Four years later, after his editor shot and killed a man, he was forced to move to New York City.

Joseph Pulitzer, photo from Wikimedia commons, public domain.

His daily paper *New York World* soon became recognized as the journal of the Democratic Party. He was known to use sensationalism to sell papers. His brilliant crowdfunding campaign raised more than $100,000 to fund the Statue of Liberty's pedestal.

In his will, Joseph Pulitzer set aside money for journalists who excel in their field. This money, which is awarded every April, is the Pulitzer Prize in journalism. To be considered for a Pulitzer Prize, one must enter the desired category and pay the $75 fee. The Columbia University School of Journalism selects the winners.

TIMELINE

1861–1865: American Civil War

1863: Emancipation Proclamation

1865, April 14: President Lincoln is shot, succumbs to injuries the next day

1865, April 21: Édouard de Laboulaye proposes France give the United States a gift

1870–1871: Franco-Prussian War

1870: Bartholdi begins to design the statue he names *La Liberté Éclairant le Monde.*

1871, June: Bartholdi visits America to meet with several wealthy and important men, hoping to gain support for the statue as he travels from New York to California. He ultimately selects Bedloe's Island as the perfect location for the statue's home.

1875: The Franco-American Union is organized. Its purpose is to raise money to build the Statue of Liberty.

1875: The first plaster model of the Statue of Liberty, standing 4½ feet (1.25) tall, is completed and unveiled at an exclusive party for 200 supporters in a Paris hotel.

1876, August: The statue's right arm and torch are completed and sent to Philadelphia for display at the Centennial Exposition.

1876, November: The right arm and torch are relocated to Madison Square Park in New York City.

1877, January: The American Committee for the construction of the pedestal is formed.

1877: The United States Congress votes to accept France's gift, but refuses to fund the project.

1877: Bedloe's Island is officially designated at the future home of the Statue of Liberty.

1878: The statue's completed head and shoulders are displayed at the Paris World Exposition.

1879: Structural engineer Eugène Viollet-de-Luc dies suddenly. Gustave Eiffel is chosen to take over the construction of the statue's inner frame.

1881: France has raised F400,000 to fund the statue's completion.

1882: The statue's arm and torch return to Paris.

1883: Jewish poet, Emma Lazarus, writes her sonnet, *The New Colossus*.

1884, January: *The New Colossus* sells at auction for $1,500.

1884: The Statue of Liberty is completely assembled outside the Paris workshop where it was designed.

1884, July 4: The Franco-American Union officially presents the Statue of Liberty to the American foreign minister to France.

1885: The Statue of Liberty is disassembled, placed in crates for transport across the Atlantic Ocean.

1885, May 21: The Statue of Liberty leaves Rouen, France, for New York City aboard the *Isere*.

1885, June 17: The Statue of Liberty arrives at Bedloe's Island.

1886, April 22: The pedestal is completed.

1886: The Statue of Liberty is reassembled on her pedestal over a period of four months. The first two rivets to be secured are named for Bartholdi and Pulitzer.

1886, October 28: President Grover Cleveland officially dedicates the Statue of Liberty on Bedloe's Island.

1886–1901: The Statue of Liberty is used as a lighthouse.

1887, November 19: Emma Lazarus dies at the age of 37.

1892: Ellis Island becomes an immigration station.

1890s: Postcards depicting the Statue of Liberty are produced and mailed to loved ones around the world. This global exposure boosts her popularity.

1897, June 14: Ellis Island Immigration Station burns down, destroying records dating back to 1855. No lives were lost in the fire.

1901–1933: The statue is placed under the care of the U.S. War Department.

1903: Emma Lazarus' poem, *The New Colossus,* is inscribed on a bronze plaque and placed on a wall inside the pedestal.

1916, July 30: Black Tom explosion in New Jersey destroys more than $20,000,000 of ammunition destined for America's World War I allies.

1924: The Statue of Liberty is designated a national monument.

1931–1937: Repairs and upgrades to the statue and the park.

1933: The National Park Service assumes care and maintenance of the Statue. Two acres of Bedloe's Island were given to the statue while the remaining 12 acres continue to be maintained by the U.S. military.

1936: The fiftieth anniversary of the Statue of Liberty. In a speech by President Theodore Roosevelt, he praised immigrants for building America and becoming its heart and soul.

1937: The National Park Service assumes responsibility over the entire island. Work is begun to make the monument more visitor friendly.

1944: Fort Wood is completely closed. The fort's remaining buildings are torn down between 1948–1950.

1946: The inside of the statue is painted with a special plastic coating, making it easier to remove graffiti.

1954: Ellis Island Immigration Processing Center is closed permanently.

1956: Bedloe's Island is renamed Liberty Island.

1957: The torch begins to stay lit all night year around.

1965: Ellis Island became part of the Statue of Liberty National Monument.

1972: The American Immigration Museum opens inside the pedestal and is closed in 1991 when Ellis Island's immigration museum opens.

1984: UNESCO designates the Statue of Liberty as a World Heritage site.

1984–1986: The Statue of Liberty is officially closed to tourists for an extensive, two-year restoration.

1986, July 3–6: "Liberty Weekend" celebration of the one hundredth birthday of the Statue of Liberty.

2001: Following the 9-11-01 terrorist attacks, Liberty Island was closed for 100 days.

2004, August: The Statue of Liberty's pedestal re-opens to the public.

2009: The crown is reopened to tourists.

2011: The Statue is closed for safety upgrades.

2011: Webcams are installed in and around the torch.

2011: One hundred twenty-fifth anniversary of the Statue of Liberty.

2012: The effects of Hurricane Sandy submerge 75 percent of Liberty Island underwater. While the surrounding buildings, docks and power were severely affected by the high winds and torrential rain, the Statue of Liberty and her pedestal suffered no damage.

2019, May: A new 26,000-square foot (2415 m²), $100-million museum opens on Liberty Island. This museum was built with funds from private citizens and corporations, including Coca Cola, Diane Von Furstenberg, Jeff Bezos and George Lucas. The Statue of Liberty Museum features three galleries. Inside, a short film explains the statue's design, fundraising efforts, building and international symbolism.

2019: The Statue of Liberty-Ellis Island Foundation creates a downloadable mobile app, which provides information about the parks and allows tourists to plan their visit.

2019: "Raising the Torch" podcast begins.

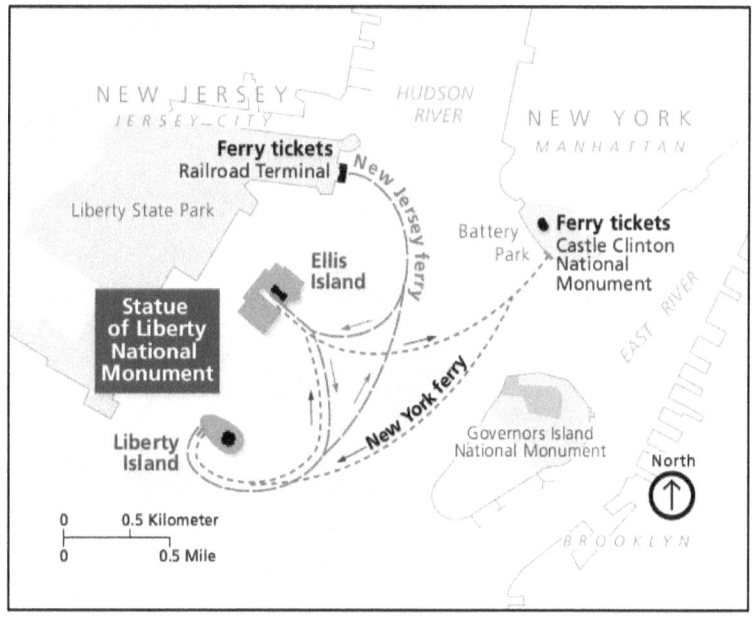

Map of ferry routes, NPS.

THE NEW COLOSSUS

★ ★ ★

Not like the brazen giant of Greek fame,
With conquering limbs astride from land to land;
Here at our sea-washed, sunset gates shall stand
A mighty woman with a torch, whose flame
Is the imprisoned lightning, and her name
Mother of Exiles. From her beacon-hand
Glows world-wide welcome; her mild eyes command
The air-bridged harbor that twin cities frame.
"Keep, ancient lands, your storied pomp!" cries she
With silent lips. "Give me your tired, your poor,
Your huddled masses yearning to breathe free,
The wretched refuse of your teeming shore.
Send these, the homeless, tempest-tost to me,
I lift my lamp beside the golden door!"

– Emma Lazarus (1883)
New York City

DID YOU KNOW...?
★ ★ ★

- In 1831, the last pirate to be hung in America, Charles Gibbs, was hung on gallows at Bedloe's Island.
- Liberty Island sees up to 25,000 daily visitors during its busiest season. Only 5,000 people can enter the pedestal, and only 500 are able to visit the crown each day.
- Water, power, and telephone service to Liberty Island is provided from New Jersey.
- Mail service to Liberty Island is provided from the Battery, Manhattan.
- The only two females present on Bedloe's Island for the October 28, 1886, dedication ceremony were Bartholdi's wife and the 13-year-old daughter of Ferdinand de Lesseps.
- The original torch rode on a float in the 1985 Rose Bowl parade.
- The company which provided the granite for the pedestal, The John Beattie Granite Company, also supplied granite for the Brooklyn Bridge's pillars.
- The Pulitzer Prize is awarded to people 21 annually.
- In 1875 Richard Morris Hunt built one of New York City's first skyscrapers, The Tribune Building.
- Frédéric Bartholdi was awarded U.S. Patent # 11,023 for the design of a statue in February 1879.
- Édouard Lefevre de Laboulaye wrote three volumes of fairy tales for his grandchildren.
- The Statue of Liberty has appeared in over 30 movies.
- Bedloe's Island was called Oyster Island by Dutch colonists.

- Bedloe Island was once a hospital for sick people.
- Black Tom was once an island bordering Bedloe's Island and Ellis Island that has been reclaimed and infilled to become part of Ellis Island.
- As part of the oxidation process, the statue first turned black prior to adopting its now-familiar blue-green patina.
- Three hundred types of hammers were used to pound the copper skin onto the wooden molds.
- The statue's copper skin and iron frame were insulated from each other by a layer of shellac and asbestos in order to prevent and chemical reactions happening between the two metals.
- The total number of stairs from the ground to the crown is 377. This number includes the few steps which approach both staircases.
- Fitted wooden molds were used to pack the copper skin of the Statue of Liberty on her trip to America to prevent the pieces from becoming misshapen.
- Ellis Island was a port of entry for more than 12 million immigrants between 1892–1954.
- During the American Revolution, the buildings on Bedloe's Island were burned by American soldiers to prevent the British from using them.
- Technically, Liberty Island is on the New Jersey side of the state line. In an 1834 land dispute, the courts awarded the city of New York ownership of the visible land of Liberty Island. New Jersey retains the submerged portions of the island and its surrounding water.
- Private boats may not dock at Liberty Island. Ferry service is available from both Manhattan, New York, and Jersey City, New Jersey to both Liberty and Ellis Islands.
- Ellis Island is nicknamed "Island of Tears" and "Heartbreak Island" because of the number of immigrants who were turned away.
- On D-Day, June 6, 1944, the Statue of Liberty's torch light flashed "V" in Morse code for "victory."
- Thomas Jefferson proposed a giant phonograph be placed inside the Statue of Liberty's head.

- Emma Lazarus' birthday is officially celebrated each year with a reading of her sonnet on Ellis Island. The poem is read by a member of the Emma Lazarus Federation of Jewish Women's Clubs, which was founded in 1944.
- Other inscriptions featured on the statue's pedestal are quotes from Presidents Woodrow Wilson, Thomas Jefferson, and Franklin D. Roosevelt, Benjamin Franklin, and Ralph Waldo Emerson as well as a passage from the Bible, Leviticus 25:10.

Photo of the back of the Statue of Liberty.
Credit: Derek Jensen 2004, Wikimedia commons

GLOSSARY OF TERMS

★ ★ ★

Abolition – to end or stop something

Abu Simbal – an ancient temple cut into a rock cliff, located in Egypt

Ally – a friend, someone with whom to cooperate to achieve a goal

Authoritarian – expecting blind submission or obedience to a leader; a government which allows little or no personal freedom

Centennial – a one-hundredth anniversary

Civil war – a war between citizens of the same country

Colonist – a member of a government-sponsored group who live in another country or area; one who starts to settle an unfamiliar territory or land

Commune – a group of people with a common purpose or who share responsibilities

Cultural diversity – having many different languages, traditions, ages, genders, religions, beliefs, and races

Debris – ruins, rubble, remains of something which has been destroyed

Democracy – government by the people; usually by election of representatives who work on the people's behalf

Disembark – to leave or step off

Emperor – a supreme ruler, often over more than one nation

Freemason/Masonic – an international group of men who help each other and others; known for secret meetings and symbolism, such as the architect's square and compass

Granite – an extremely hard, durable but porous rock which is made of crystal formations containing quartz

Iconic – to be a symbol or representation of something else

Immigrant – a person who leaves one country to live in another

Innate – inborn, natural

Legislators – one who writes and/or passes laws

Monarchy – a royal family; a nation ruled by a king and/or queen

Persecution – to be harassed, cruelly, or unfairly treated due to a difference in religion, gender, political association, or race

Republic – citizens elected by the people who govern the nation according to an agreed-upon set of rules, such as the Constitution

Rivets – a short metal pin used to hold items together

Solicit – to ask or request

Somber – gloomy, dull, or unhappy mood

QUESTIONS FROM THE BOOK

★ ★ ★

1. What country proposed a gift to the United States?
2. What was the reason for this gift?
3. What war had the United States recently fought?
4. Who or what was the Statue of Liberty modeled after?
5. What is the official name of the Statue of Liberty?
6. What famous engineer designed and built the inner skeleton?
2. What part of the statue was placed on display to help pay for the pedestal? Where was it displayed?
3. What part did Joseph Pulitzer play in fundraising?
4. Why was copper chosen for the statue's outer skin?
5. What is the significance or meaning behind the crown's rays? The broken chains?
6. What was the name of Emma Lazarus's poem? Why was it written?

BIBLIOGRAPHY

Bartholdi, Frédéric Auguste. Trans. By Rodman Gilder. *Frédéric Auguste Bartholdi Papers (1871). The New York Public Library Archives and Transcripts.* 2019. http://archives.nypl.org/mss/223, retrieved November 13, 2019.

Bartholdi, Frédéric Auguste. The Statue of Liberty Enlightening the World. New York: North American Review, 1885.

Bendix, Aria. "The Statue of Liberty Has Been Missing Its Original 3,600-pound Torch for 35 Years." *Business Insider US,* July 5, 2019. https://www.businessinsider.com/statue-of-liberty-torch-museum-2019-5, retrieved November 13, 2019.

Blanchet, Christian and Bertrand Dard. *The Statue of Liberty.* n.c.: New Word City, 2017.

Bracci, Chelsea. "Lady Liberty's Kickstarter Campaign of the 1880s." *American Jewish Historical Society*, July 11, 2019. http://www.ajhs.org/blog/lady-libertys-kickstarter-campaign-1880s, retrieved November 13, 2019.

Brockell, Gillian. "The Statue of Liberty Was Created to Celebrate Freed Slaves, Not Immigrants, Its New Museum Recounts." *The Washington Post*, May 23, 2019. https://www.washingtonpost.com/history/2019/05/23/statue-liberty-was-created-celebrate-freed-slaves-not-immigrants/, retrieved November 13, 2019.

Cartwright, Mark. "Colossus of Rhodes." *Ancient History Encyclopedia*, July 25, 2018. https://www.ancient.eu/Colossus_of_Rhodes/, retrieved November 13, 2019.

"Conservation-restoration of the Statue of Liberty." *Wikipedia: the Free Encyclopedia*, November 8, 2019. https://en.wikipedia.org/wiki/Conservation-restoration_of_the_Statue_of_Liberty, retrieved November 13, 2019.

Euler, Heinrich Gustav. Napoleon III. Encyclopædia Britannica, 2019. https://www. britannica.com/biography/Napoleon-III-emperor-of-France, retrieved November 13, 2019.

Fletcher, Richard. "Scottish Rite Journal" as cited in "National Treasure, The Freemasons, Mt. Rushmore, and the Statue of Liberty." *Copasetic Flow.Blogspot.com,* March 12, 2009. https://copaseticflow.blogspot.com/2008/03/national-treasure-freemasons-mt.html, retrieved November 13, 2019.

"From Concept to Construction to Installation—Facts and Figures." *Copper Development Association Inc.* https://www.copper.org/education/liberty/liberty_design3.html, retrieved November 13, 2019.

"From Sea to Shining Sea: The Story of L'Isere and Miss Liberty." *Francaisdeletranger.org*: The Official Website of the Movement of French Abroad, May 26, 2016. http://www.francaisdeletranger.org/en/2016/05/22/mdfdeusa-from-sea-to-shining-sea-the-story-of-lisere-and-miss-liberty-mdfdejesuisladyliberty130-nps100/, retrieved November 13, 2019.

Glass, Andrew. "President Cleveland Dedicates the Statue of Liberty, October 28, 1886." *Politico.com,* October 28, 2011. https://www.politico.com/story/2011/10/president-cleveland-dedicates-the-statue-of-liberty-oct-28-1886-067004, retrieved November 13, 2019.

Hayden, Richard Seth et al. *Restoring the Statue of Liberty: Sculpture, Structure, Symbol.* New York: McGraw-Hill, 1986.

Hingston, Sandy. "10 Things You Might Not Know About the 1876 Centennial Exhibition." *Philadelphia News*, May 10, 2016.https://www.phillymag.com/news/2016/05/10/ centennial-exhibition-history/, retrieved November 13, 2019.

History.com Editors. Statue of Liberty. *A&E Televisions Networks, LLC*, December 2, 2009-July 1, 2019. www.history.com/topics/landmarks/statue-of-liberty, retrieved November 13, 2019.

Holub, Joan, *What Is the Statue of Liberty?* New York: Grosset and Dunlap, 2014.

"Improvements in the Statue Since 1886." *The National Park Service*, September 25, 2000. https://www.nps.gov/parkhistory/online_books/hh/11/hh11k.htm, retrieved November 13, 2019.

Kiger, Patrick J. "Statue of Liberty: The Making of an Icon." *A&E Televisions Networks, LLC,* May 14, 2019. https://www.history.com/news/statue-of-liberty-icon-building, retrieved November 13, 2019.

Mancini, Mark. "The Story Behind the Poem on the Statue of Liberty." *MentalFloss.com*, July 4, 2018. http://mentalfloss.com/article/92248/story-behind-poem-statue-liberty, retrieved November 13, 2019.

Maurer, C. "The Statue of Liberty and Masonry: Grand Master Charles Singer, New York." *Academia*, 2019. https://www.academia.edu/12613241/The_Statue_of_Liberty_and_Masonry_Grand_Master_Charles_Singer_New_York, retrieved November 13, 2019.

Noguès, Olivier. "Auguste Bartholdi," *Landmarks of the World,* 2013-2019. https://www. wonders-of-the-world.net/Statue-of-Liberty/Auguste-Bartholdi.php, retrieved November 13, 2019.

"History of the Statue of Liberty," *Landmarks of the World,* 2013-2019. https://www.wonders-of-the-world.net/Statue-of-Liberty/History-of-the-statue-of-Liberty.php

"Philadelphia, United States 1876: Centennial International Exhibition." *America's Best History*, 2019. https://americasbesthistory.com/wfphiladelphia1876.html, retrieved November 13, 2019.

Rivers, Justin. History: "The Cornerstone of the Statue of Liberty's Pedestal Is Placed." *Untapped New York,* August 3, 2016. https://untappedcities.com/2016/08/03/this-week-in-nyc-history-the-cornerstone-of-the-statue-of-libertys-pedestal-is-placed/, retrieved November 13, 2019.

Rosenberg, Jennifer. "The Colossus at Rhodes: One of the Seven Wonders of the Ancient World." *Thought.Co,* May 30, 2019. https://www.thoughtco.com/the-colossus-at-rhodes-1434531, retrieved November 13, 2019.

"Statue of Liberty and Liberty Island Improvements, New York, NY." *The Living New Deal.* https://livingnewdeal.org/projects/statue-of-liberty-new-york-ny/, retrieved November 13, 2019.

Statue of Liberty Museum, 2016, https://www.libertyellisfoundation.org/statueoflibertymuseum, retrieved November 13, 2019.

"Statue of Liberty, NY." *Lighthousefriends.com,* 2001-2019. https://lighthousefriends.com/ light.asp?ID=581, retrieved November 13, 2019.

"The Statue of Liberty and America's Crowdfunding Pioneer." *BBC News Magazine*, April 25, 2013. https://www.bbc.com/news/magazine-21932675, retrieved November 13, 2019.

Thomas, M. "Statue of Liberty." Purdue University Materials Engineering, 2018. https://engineering.purdue.edu/MSE/aboutus/gotmaterials/Parks/thomas.html, retrieved November 13, 2019.

Young, Michelle. "See the Site Where the Statue of Liberty Was Built in Paris." *Untapped New York*, July 10, 2018. https://untappedcities.com/2018/07/10/see-the-site-where-the-statue-of-liberty-was-built-in-paris/, retrieved November 13, 2019.

NOTES

ALSO BY JANICE WILHELM

★ ★ ★

Love Came Down, Unwrapping the Gift of Our Risen Savior

ePUB ISBN: 978-1-7327803-2-3
MOBI ISBN: 978-1-7327803-1-6
Paperback ISBN: 978-1-7327803-0-9

The Birth of Jesus Christmas Coloring Book
ISBN: 978-1-729-22175-4

A Vintage Christmas Coloring Book
ISBN: 978-1-790-47694-7

Coming Soon! Expected publication date early 2021:

The Christian Living Series

Social Media Links:

Website:

https://www.wildrose-media.com

Facebook:

https://www.facebook.com/janicewilhelmauthor/

https://facebook.com/WRM2019/

Email:

PUBLISHER: https://wildrosemedia18@gmail.com

AUTHOR: https://janicewilhelmauthor@gmail.com

Sign up for email notifications. Be among the first to learn the latest news- including new releases, current works in progress, and to receive exclusive offers and coupon codes.

www.ingramcontent.com/pod-product-compliance
Lightning Source LLC
Chambersburg PA
CBHW031123080526
44587CB00011B/1086